Search and Find
DINOSAURS

Claire Stamper

ARCTURUS

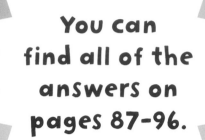

You can find all of the answers on pages 87-96.

There is a pronunciation guide on page 86.

ARCTURUS

This edition published in 2020 by Arcturus Publishing Limited
26/27 Bickels Yard, 151–153 Bermondsey Street,
London SE1 3HA

Copyright © Arcturus Holdings Limited

Illustrations by Claire Stamper
Design by Ms Mousepenny & Rosie Bellwood
Written by Lisa Regan
Edited by Sebastian Rydberg & Violet Peto

ISBN: 978-1-78950-250-3
CH006949NT
Supplier 29, Date 0120, Print run 8265

Printed in China

3

Find three of these spiral ammonites among the dinosaurs.

Find three Parasaurolophus who look just like this one.

Find two Stegosaurus that are blue and green.

Find two Triceratops that are purple and blue.

Which T. rex is covered in polka dots?

How many T. rex are wearing mittens?

Which mighty creature has blue eyes?

Which bone does not look like any of the others?

How many purple Suchomimus like this can you find?

Find two more of this purple, flying Pteranodon.

Find two dinosaurs matching this red one.

Find three Ankylosaurus just like this one.

11

Find the Allosaurus with blue eyes.

Where is the Allosaurus with no teeth?

Which Allosaurus is carrying a spiky potplant?

How many Allosaurus have stripes?

13

Which Pachycephalosaurus is yellow with blue stripes?

How many dinosaurs have green markings?

Find the dinosaur with a crash helmet on.

Look for an animal with very large teeth!

14

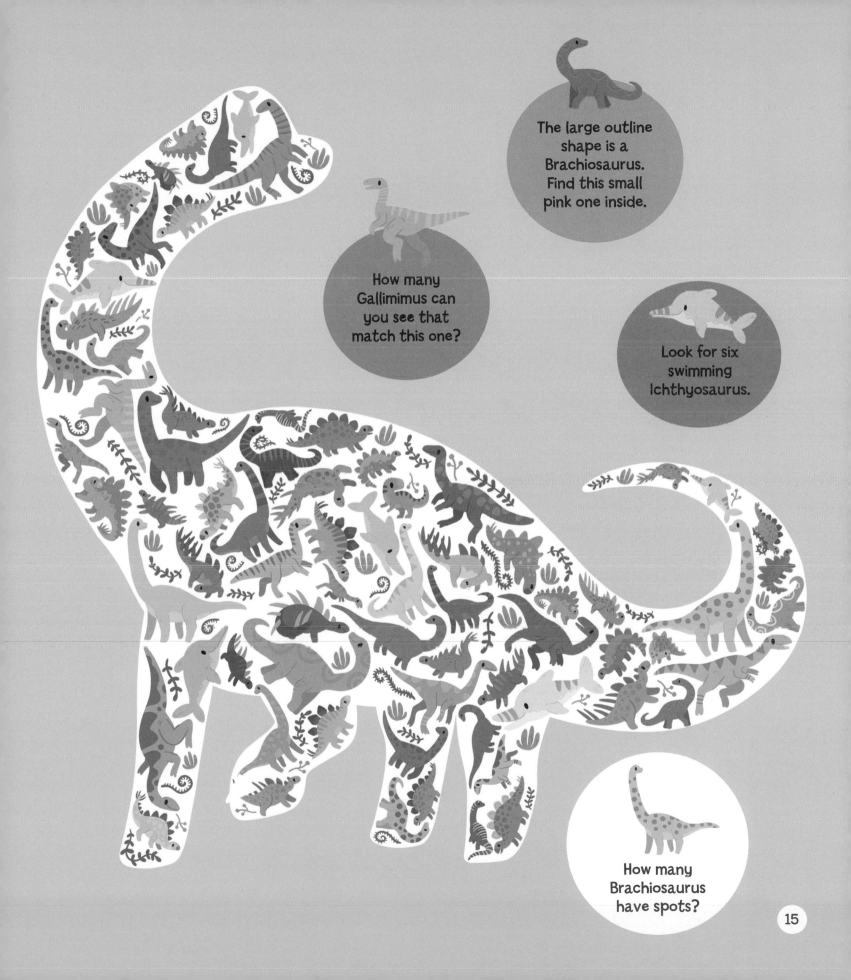

The large outline shape is a Brachiosaurus. Find this small pink one inside.

How many Gallimimus can you see that match this one?

Look for six swimming Ichthyosaurus.

How many Brachiosaurus have spots?

15

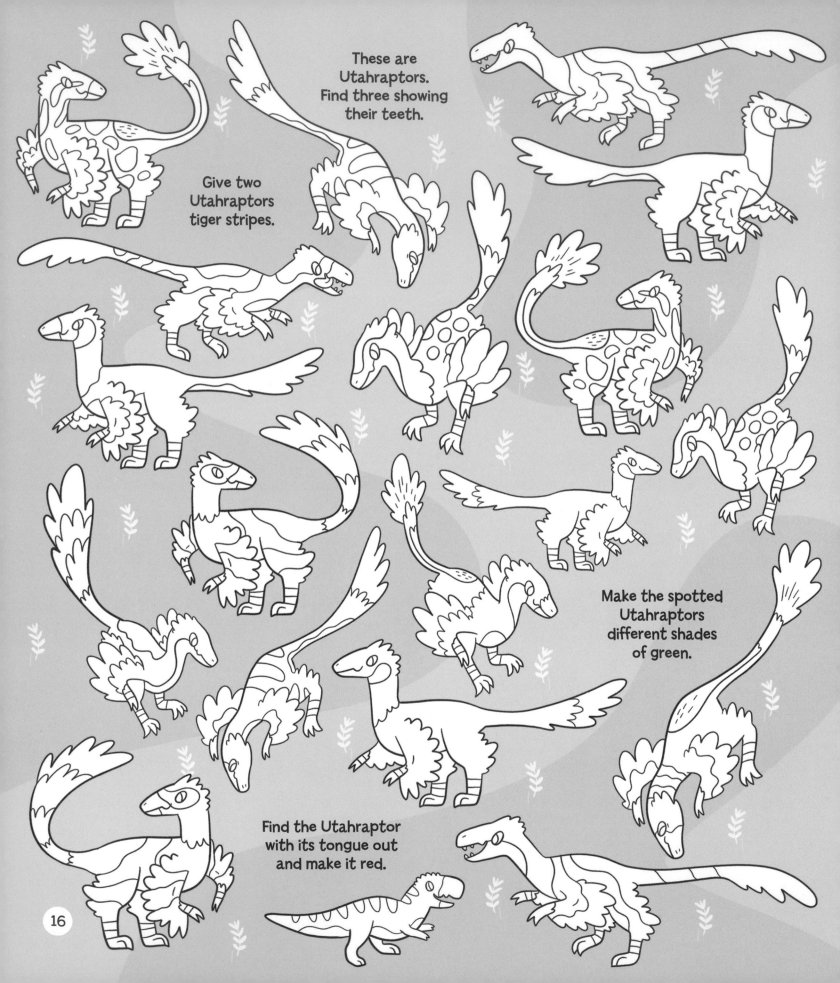

These are Utahraptors. Find three showing their teeth.

Give two Utahraptors tiger stripes.

Make the spotted Utahraptors different shades of green.

Find the Utahraptor with its tongue out and make it red.

16

Find the only
red Spinosaurus
in the crowd.

How many
Parasaurolophus
can you see that
match this one?

Find two green
spotted Triceratops
that look just like
this one.

Find two
cycads in
the main
shape.

Look for a Stegosaurus in socks.

Can you spy a dinosaur in a bow-tie?

Find the biggest dragonfly on the page.

Where is the horned rhinoceros beetle?

Which Ankylosaurus has an unusual tail club?

Which Ankylosaurus is wearing a watch?

Find the Ankylosaurus with purple spikes.

How many Ankylosaurus have green legs?

19

Can you find two of these green sauropods?

Find two dino heads that look like this one.

Can you find my spotted tricera-twin?

How many blue Microraptors like this one are inside the main shape?

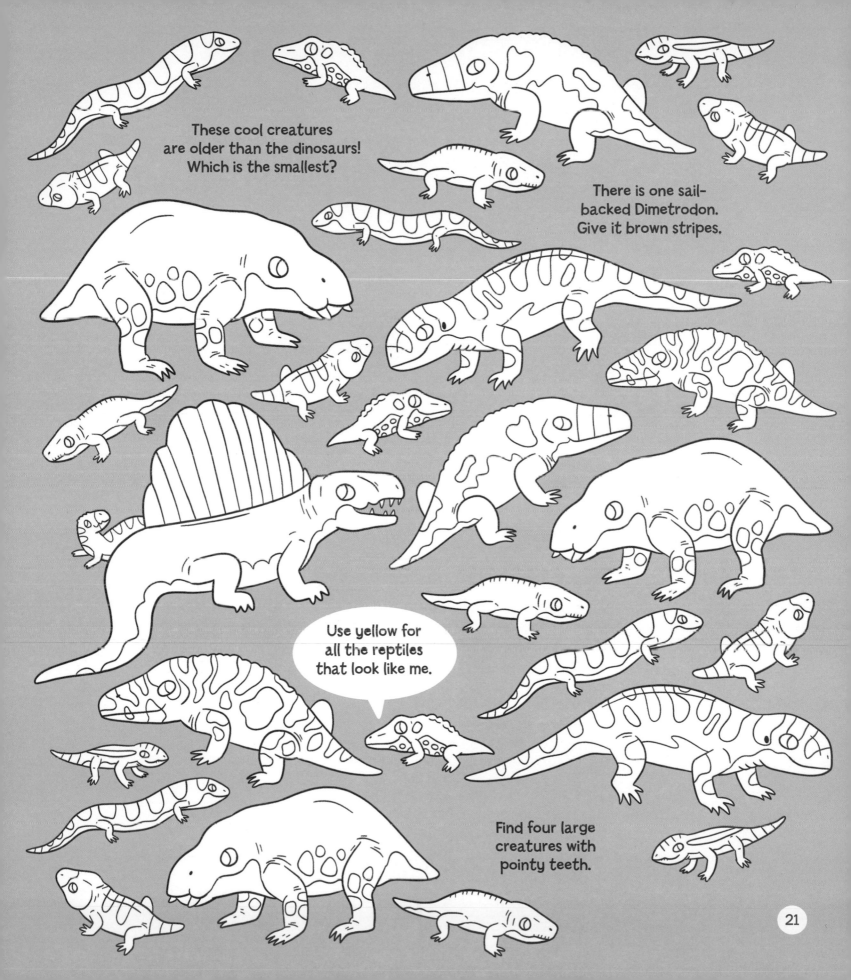

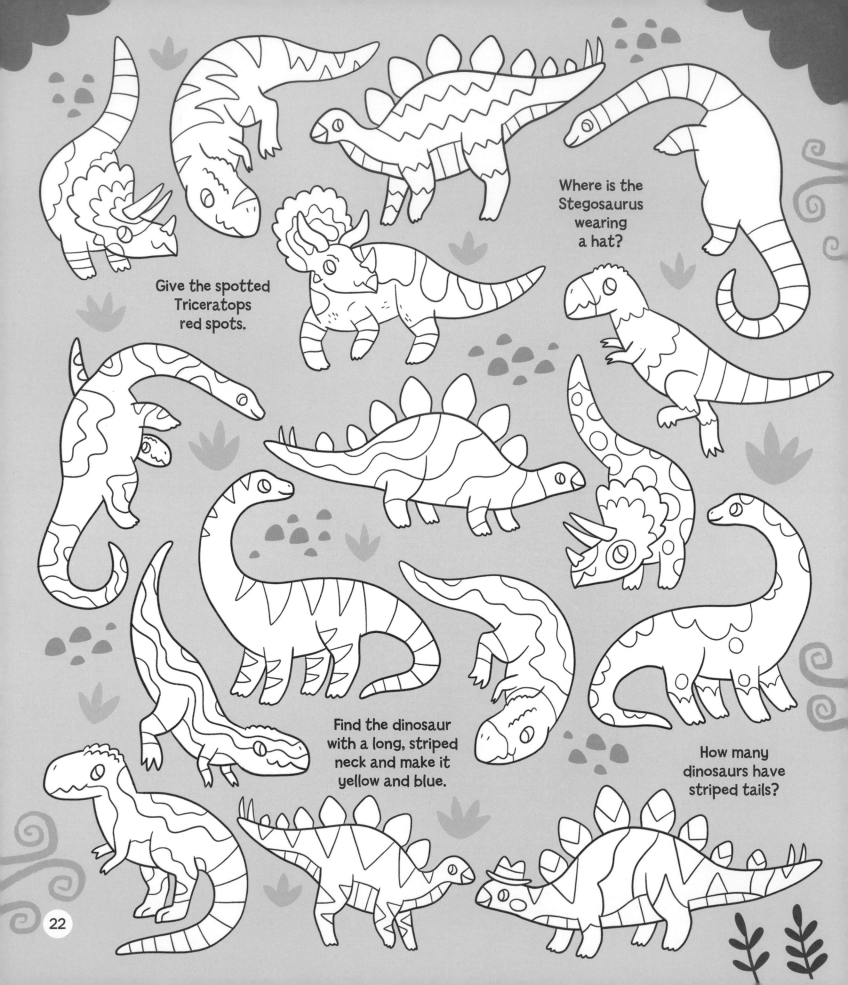

Where is the Stegosaurus wearing a hat?

Give the spotted Triceratops red spots.

Find the dinosaur with a long, striped neck and make it yellow and blue.

How many dinosaurs have striped tails?

22

23

Which big Brachiosaurus has the shortest tail?

Which little Dryosaurus has stripes on its back?

Can you find the dinosaur wearing glasses?

Find a baby Brachiosaurus next to its mother.

24

Can you find two blue Pachycephalosaurus matching this one?

How many spotted Parasaurolophus can you spot in the crowd?

The large shape is a Torosaurus. How many small ones are hidden inside the outline?

Find six flying reptiles with their beaks open.

Use red and black for tails like mine.

Find the strangest beaks and shade them orange.

How many toothed creatures can you count?

Give the spotty flyers blue spots.

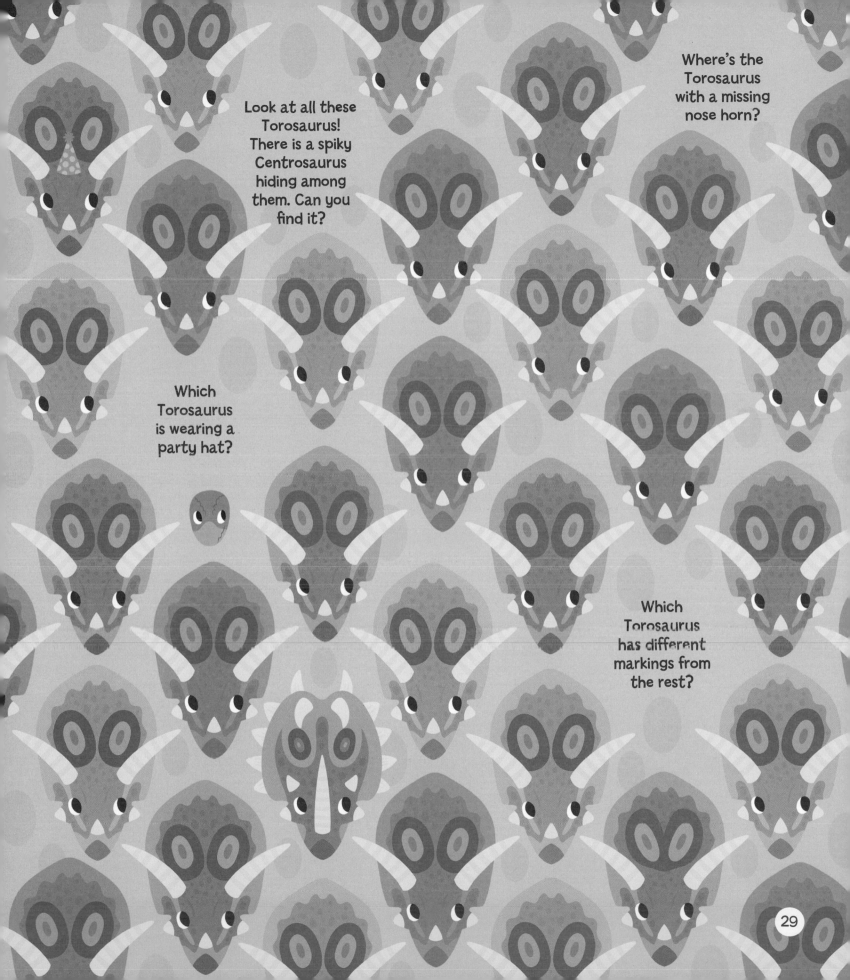

Look at all these Torosaurus! There is a spiky Centrosaurus hiding among them. Can you find it?

Where's the Torosaurus with a missing nose horn?

Which Torosaurus is wearing a party hat?

Which Torosaurus has different markings from the rest?

29

Can you find three blue dinosaurs just like this one?

Find this green, spiky-tailed Kentrosaurus in the crowd.

Count all of the spotted creatures.

Which dinosaur is wearing a coat?

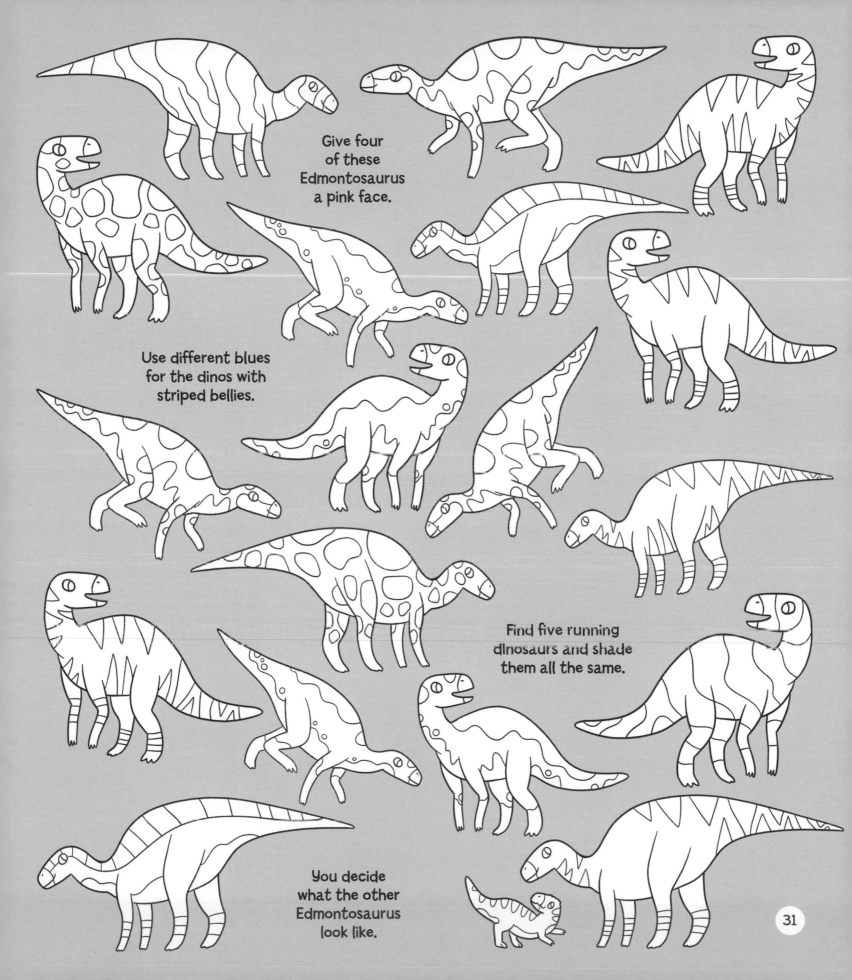

Give four
of these
Edmontosaurus
a pink face.

Use different blues
for the dinos with
striped bellies.

Find five running
dinosaurs and shade
them all the same.

You decide
what the other
Edmontosaurus
look like.

31

How many of these green Acrocanthosaurus are there?

Find four long-necked sauropods mixed up with all the meat-eaters.

Find two other Carnotaurus with horns like mine.

Can you spot the dino with long, green spikes on its head?

Who has the curliest tail?

Who has a yellow head crest?

Which two dinosaurs are exactly the same?

Can you spy someone with an orange eye?

33

One Allosaurus in this herd has an eyeglass. Can you find it?

Which footprint is different from the rest?

How many of them have red stripes?

Where is the Allosaurus with red spots?

34

Look for the only purple flying creature.

The outline shape is a Corythosaurus. Can you find one inside with a striped tail?

Find a Suchomimus similar to this one, with a fish in its mouth.

Find the yellow, swimming reptile with a long neck.

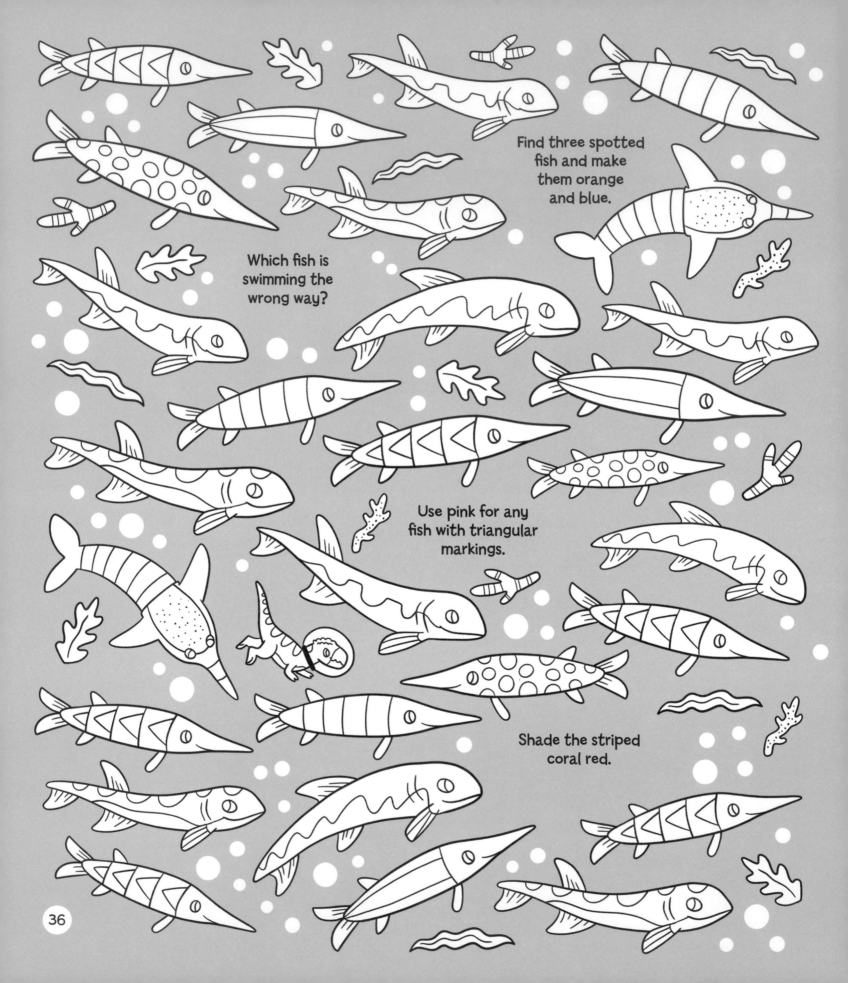

Find three spotted fish and make them orange and blue.

Which fish is swimming the wrong way?

Use pink for any fish with triangular markings.

Shade the striped coral red.

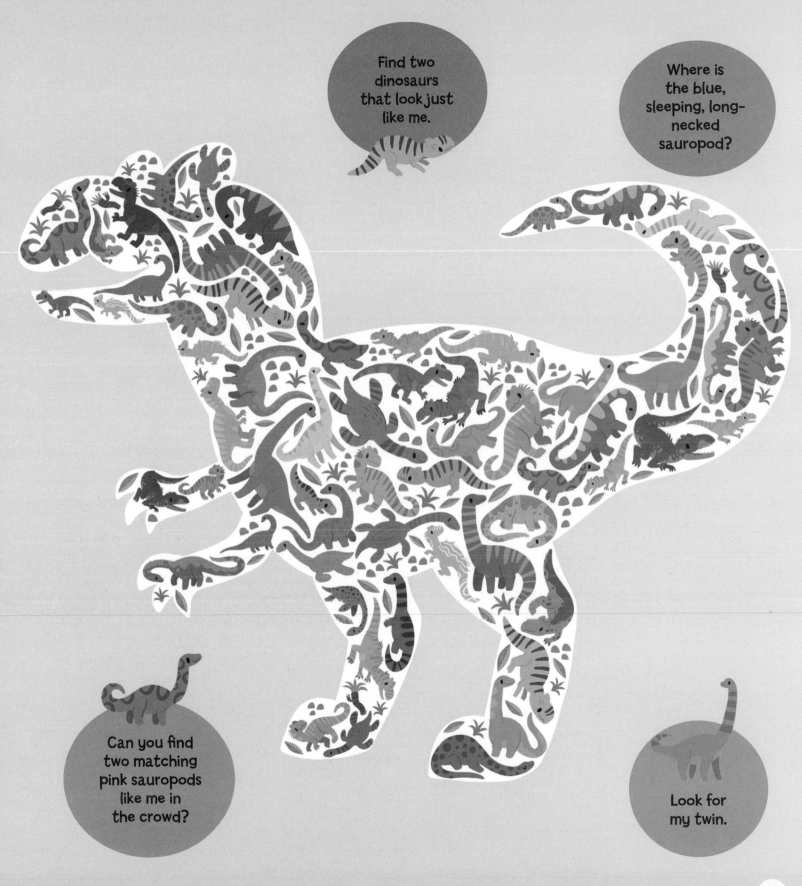

How many
Deinonychus have
their mouths open?

Find three
dinosaurs with
yellow beaks.

Can you find a
fallen feather?

Which
Deinonychus
has a crown on
its head?

39

Find the only flying creature with wings hidden in the main shape.

How many Ichthyosaurus are there?

Can you find two crocodile-shaped Kronosaurus matching this one?

How many pink nautilus are there?

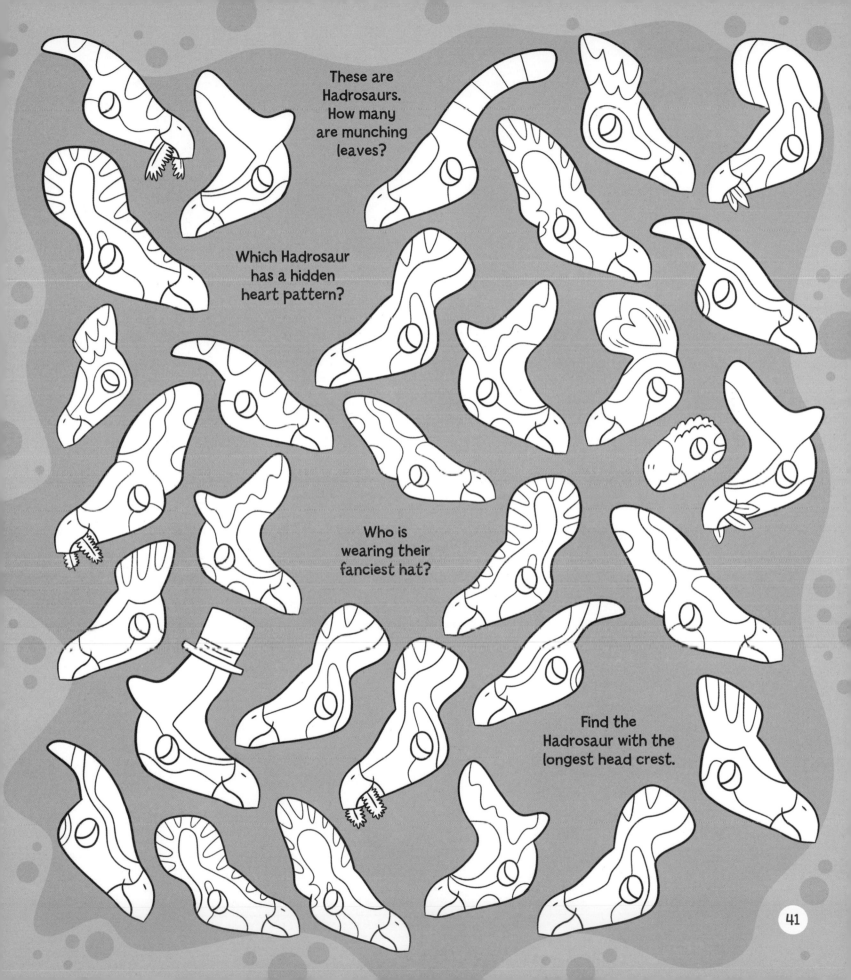

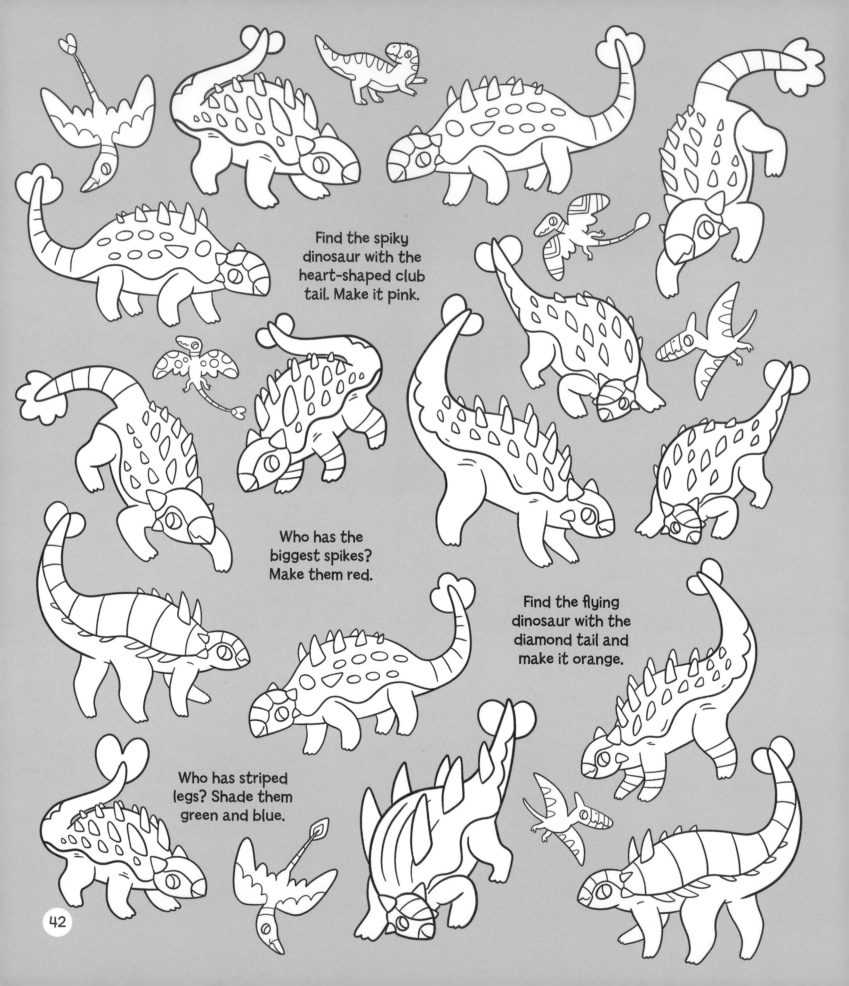

Find the spiky dinosaur with the heart-shaped club tail. Make it pink.

Who has the biggest spikes? Make them red.

Find the flying dinosaur with the diamond tail and make it orange.

Who has striped legs? Shade them green and blue.

42

Which dinosaur has a lizard lunch?

Who is waving a magic wand?

Which dinosaur has spots and no stripes?

Can you find the two tiny lizards that look exactly the same?

43

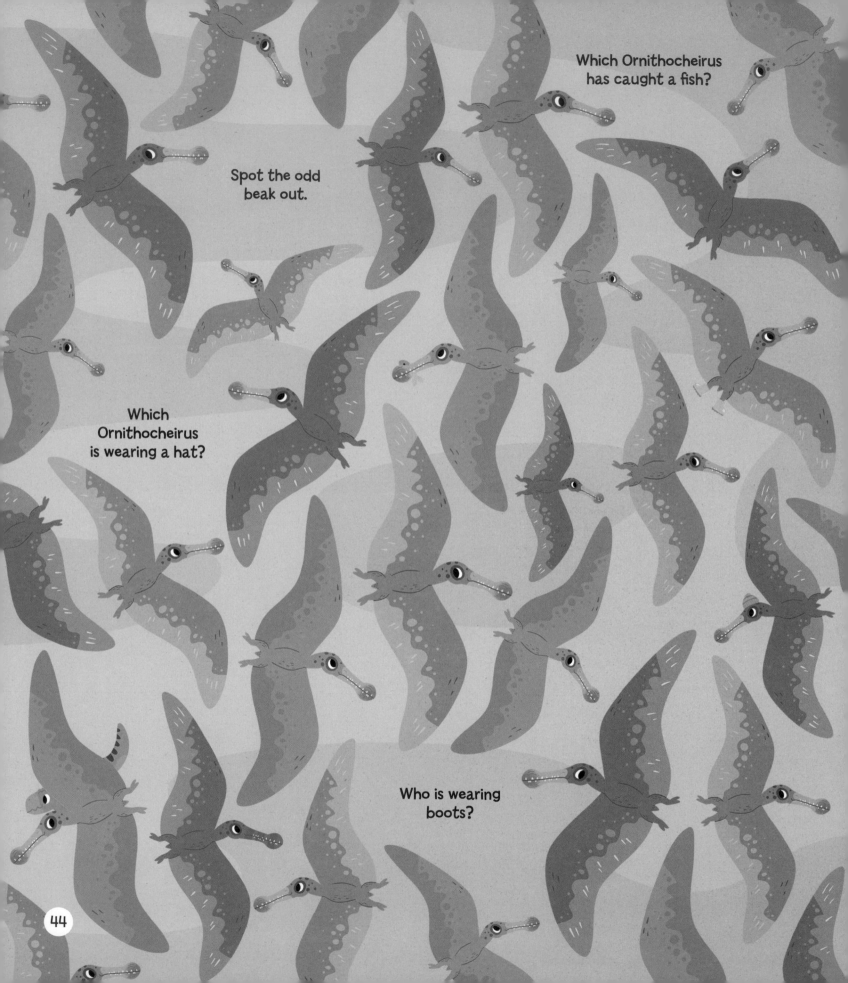

Which Ornithocheirus has caught a fish?

Spot the odd beak out.

Which Ornithocheirus is wearing a hat?

Who is wearing boots?

44

How many fish are there?

Look for a dinosaur with its tail in a twist.

Find the dinosaur munching on leaves inside the main shape.

Count all of the dinosaurs that have a neck frill, like this one.

Use blue for the Velociraptor with a feathered head crest.

Which Velociraptor has unusual eyes?

How many lizards have a curly tail?

Give three Velociraptors pink tails.

46

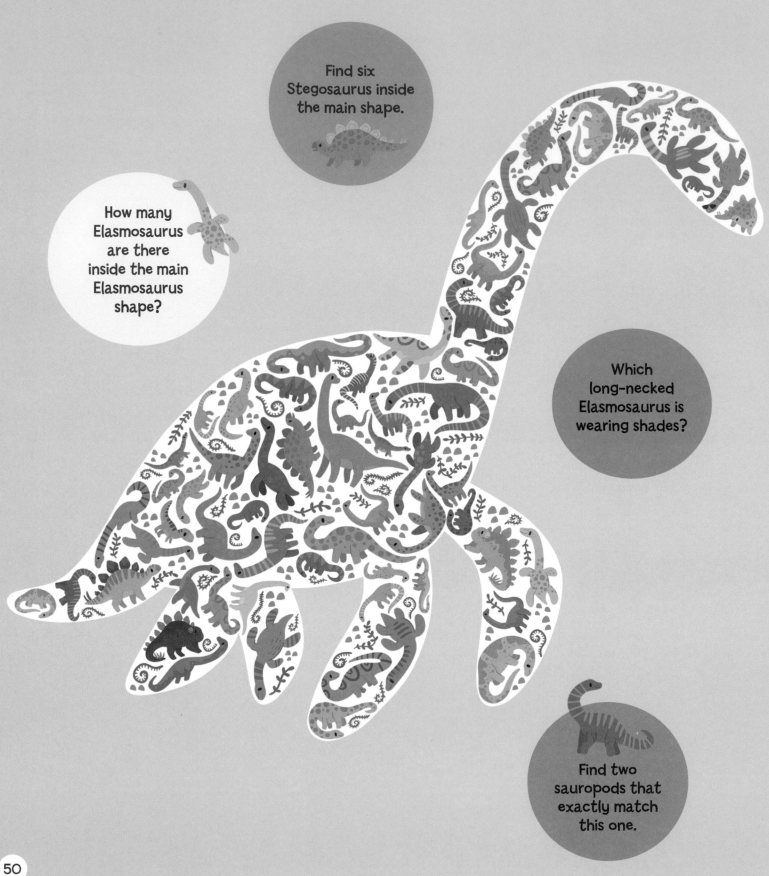

Find six Stegosaurus inside the main shape.

How many Elasmosaurus are there inside the main Elasmosaurus shape?

Which long-necked Elasmosaurus is wearing shades?

Find two sauropods that exactly match this one.

Find the joker wearing a disguise.

Sort the flowers into fives and shade each group differently.

Which Apatosaurus has the curliest tail?

Use blue on three Apatosaurus.

51

Which Iguanodon is wearing gloves?

Find a flying creature with a hat on.

Look for a small furry mammal scuttling around.

How many flying creatures can you count?

Which of these Lambeosaurus has spots instead of stripes?

How many dinosaurs have a plain head crest?

Who has a spotted head crest?

Someone's dropped their watch. Can you find it?

Find two Brachiosaurus with very long necks.

Find two Kentrosaurus that match this one.

Find this pink Kentrosaurus with green spikes.

Spot three Triceratops with pink stripes like this one.

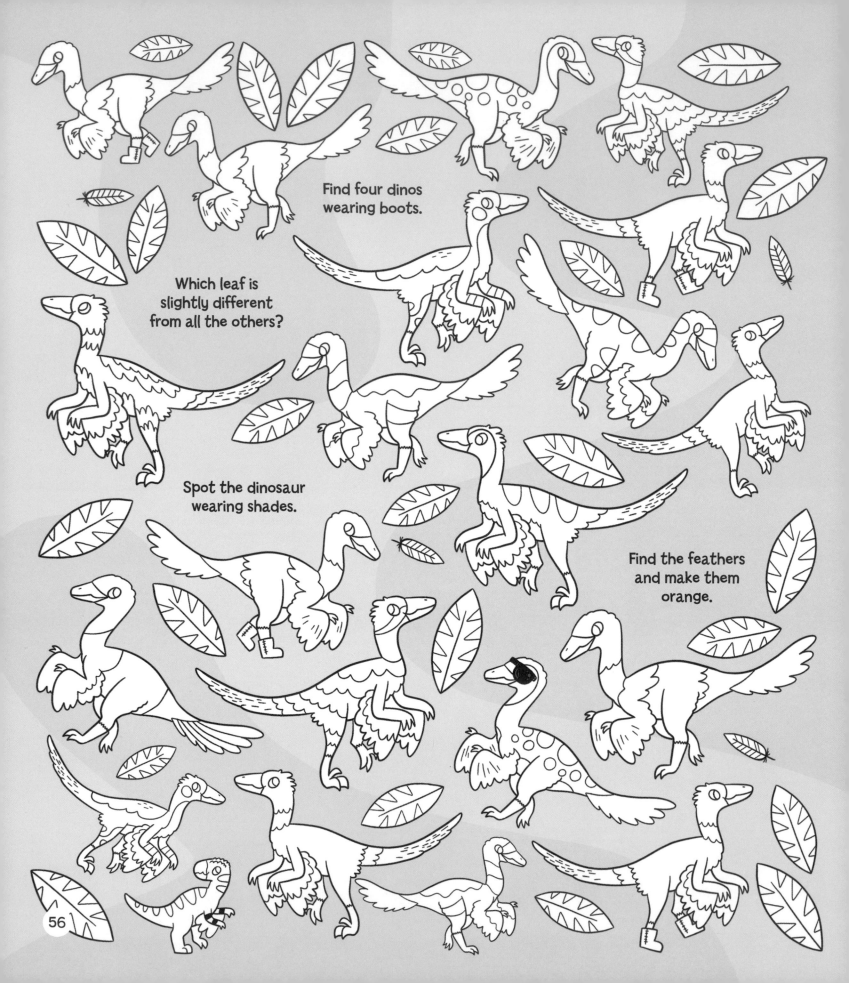

Find four dinos wearing boots.

Which leaf is slightly different from all the others?

Spot the dinosaur wearing shades.

Find the feathers and make them orange.

How many Triceratops inside the main shape are blue?

How many unhatched eggs can you find?

How many orange flyers are there?

Find the baby just hatched from its egg.

Which of these Euoplocephalus has its shoulder spikes missing?

How many Euoplocephalus have a green club on their tail?

Who is wearing a stylish scarf?

How many dinosaurs have a spotted underside?

59

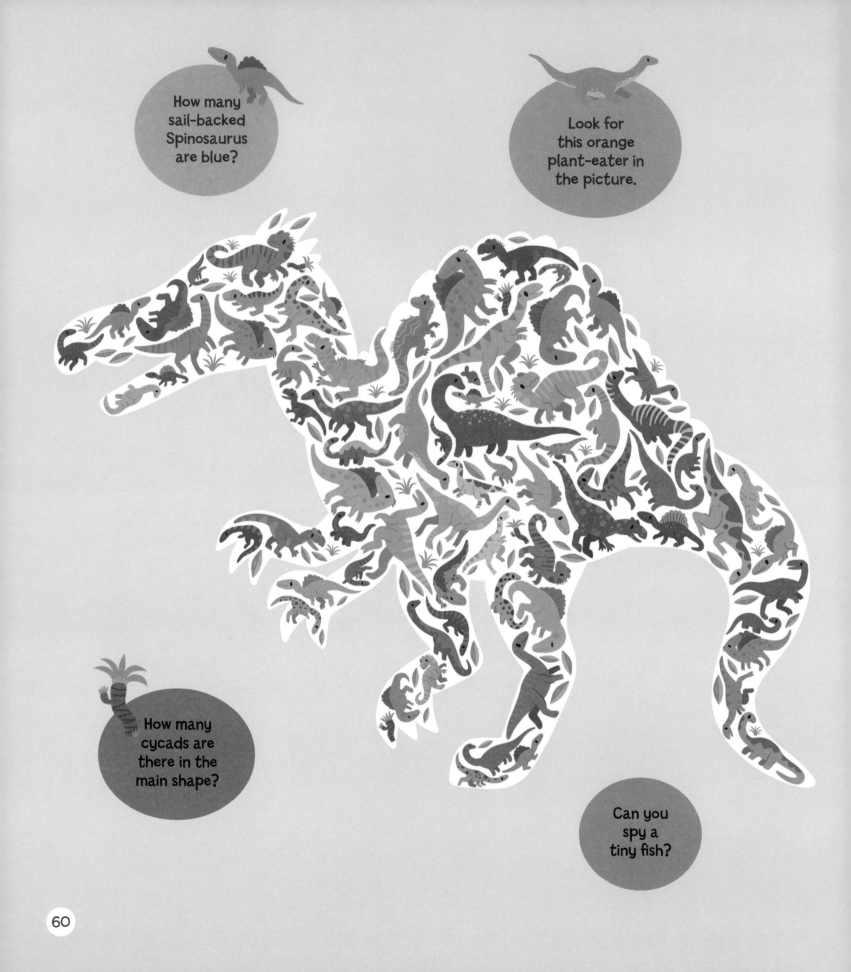

How many sail-backed Spinosaurus are blue?

Look for this orange plant-eater in the picture.

How many cycads are there in the main shape?

Can you spy a tiny fish?

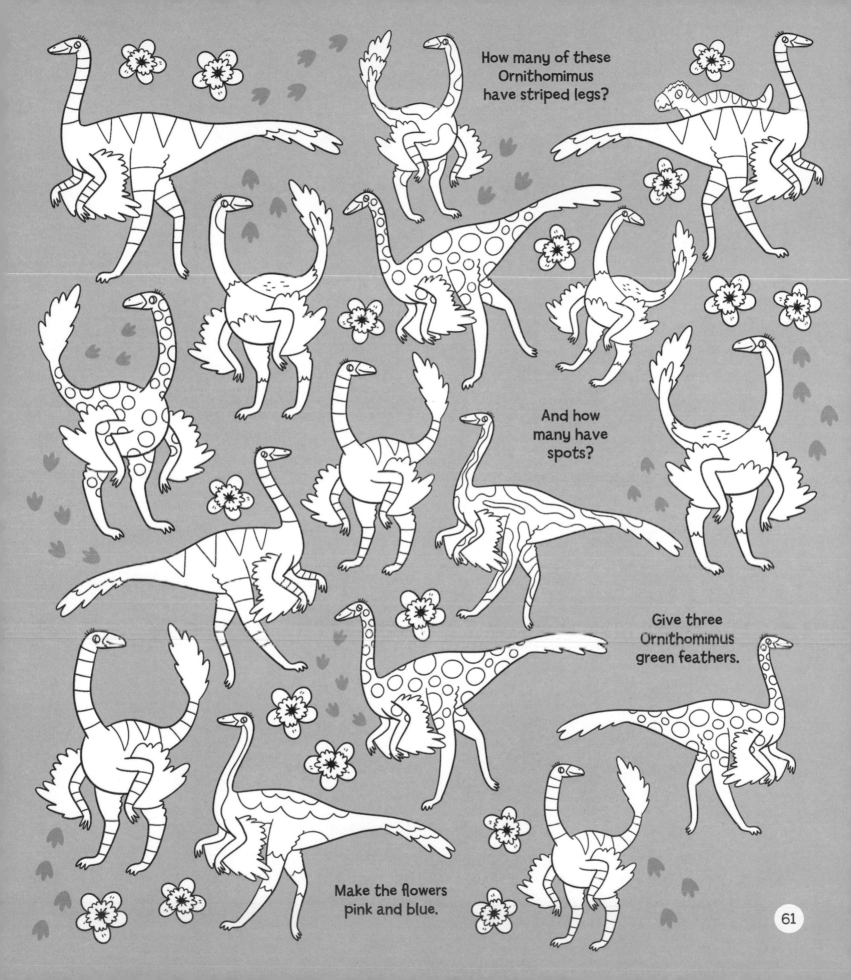

How many of these Ornithomimus have striped legs?

And how many have spots?

Give three Ornithomimus green feathers.

Make the flowers pink and blue.

61

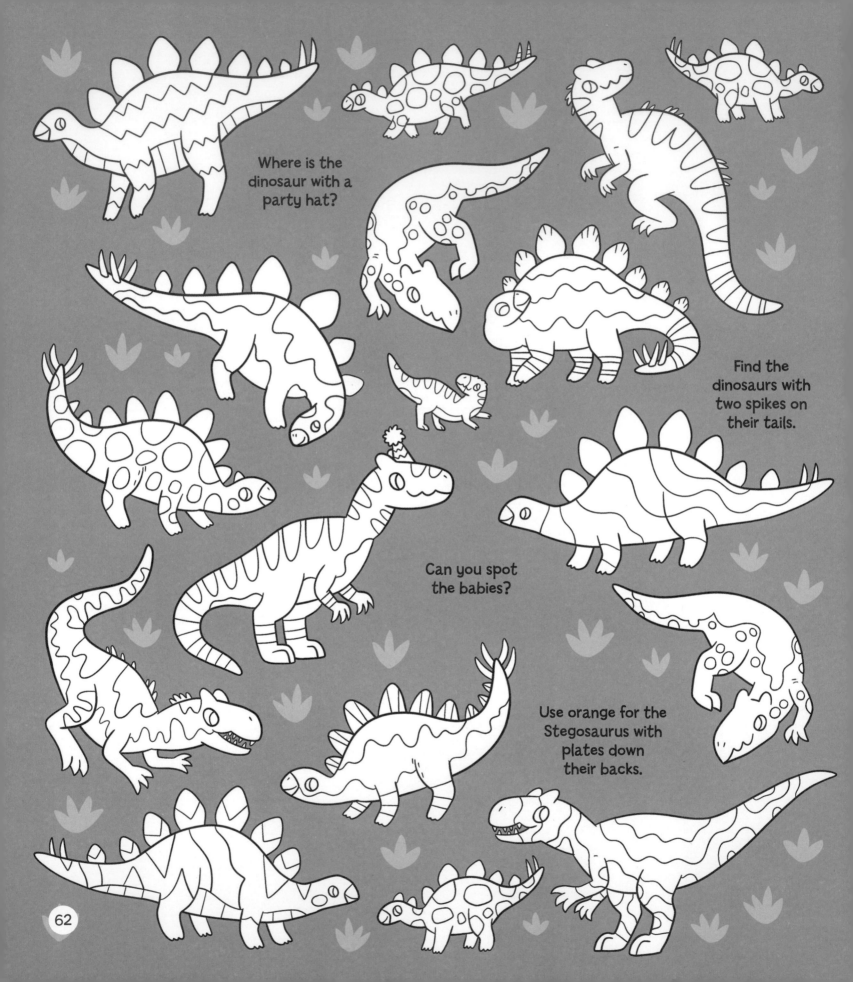

Where is the dinosaur with a party hat?

Find the dinosaurs with two spikes on their tails.

Can you spot the babies?

Use orange for the Stegosaurus with plates down their backs.

Find three Rhamphorhynchus with yellow wings.

Which Rhamphorhynchus has orange eyes?

Find the Rhamphorhynchus carrying a stick.

Which Rhamphorhynchus is missing its sharp teeth?

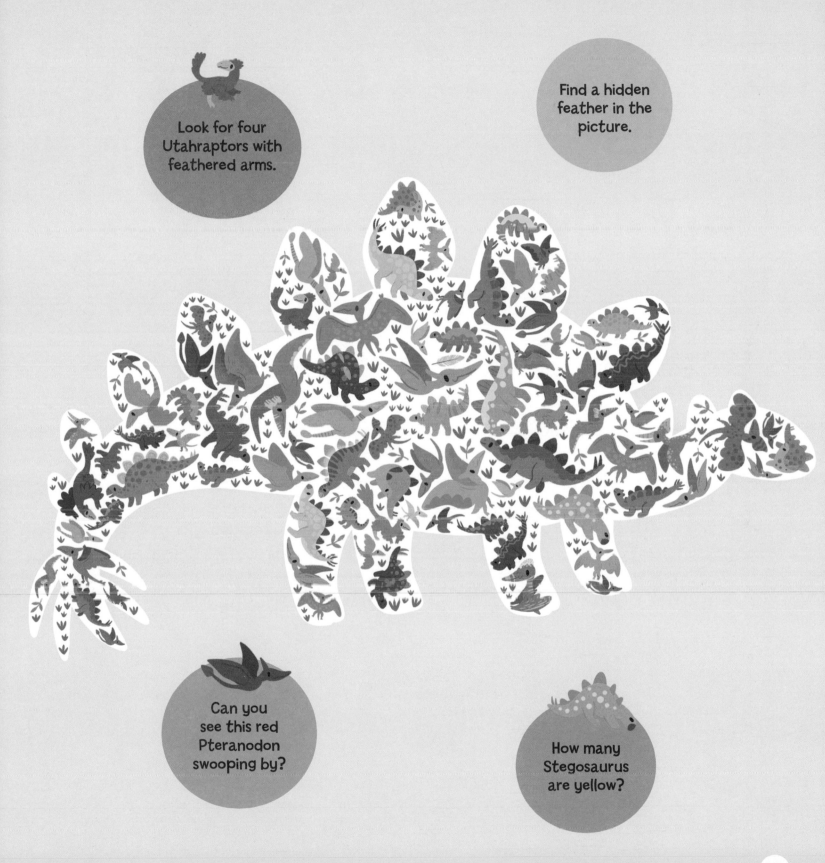

Look for four Utahraptors with feathered arms.

Find a hidden feather in the picture.

Can you see this red Pteranodon swooping by?

How many Stegosaurus are yellow?

65

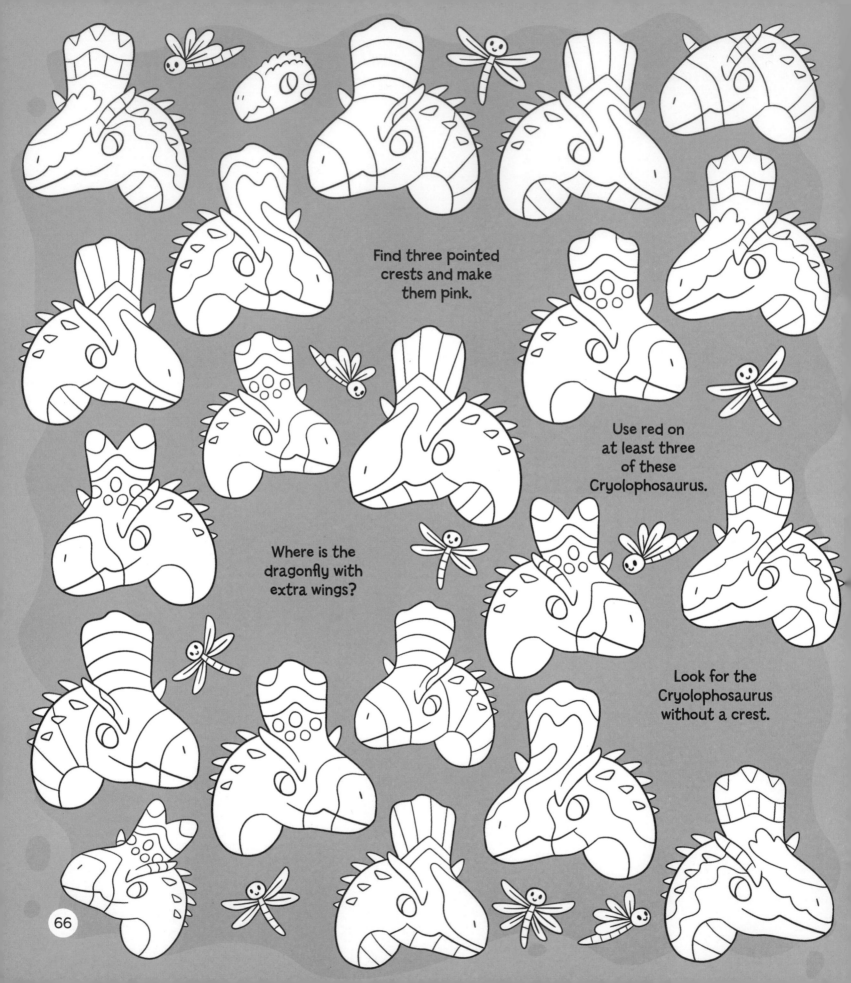

Find three pointed crests and make them pink.

Use red on at least three of these Cryolophosaurus.

Where is the dragonfly with extra wings?

Look for the Cryolophosaurus without a crest.

Can you find the dragonfly?

Find a dinosaur with a striped tail.

Which flying pterosaur has caught a fish?

How many horned Styracosaurus can you count?

67

Find five
little lizards.

Which
dinosaur has
a toy dino?

Who has a blue
tail club?

Look for a
nest with four
eggs in it.

68

Where is the turtle hiding?

Which large Cryptoclidus has an S shape on its back?

Find four fish in the water.

How many Cryptoclidus have stripes?

How many spiky
Kentrosaurus can
you see?

Look for three green
Pachycephalosaurus.

Find the
dinosaur
with no tail.

Can you
see a cycad
inside the
main shape?

70

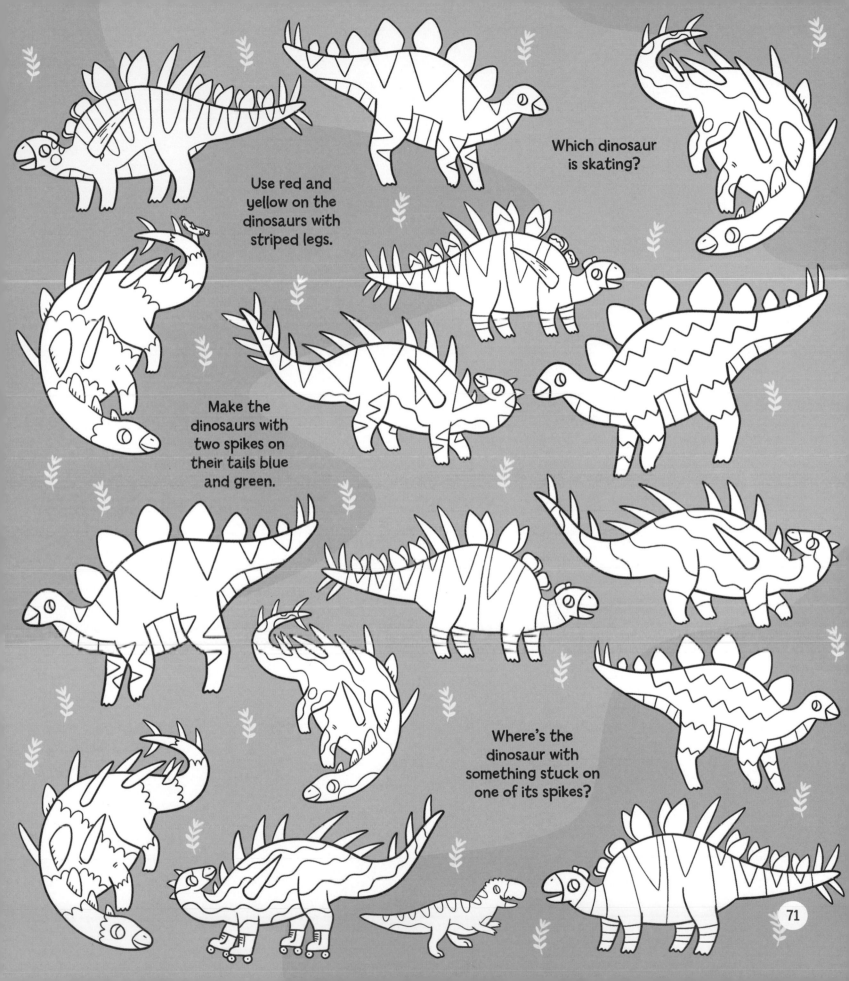

Use red and yellow on the dinosaurs with striped legs.

Which dinosaur is skating?

Make the dinosaurs with two spikes on their tails blue and green.

Where's the dinosaur with something stuck on one of its spikes?

71

Where is the Lambeosaurus with no head crest?

How many have leg stripes?

Can you spot the beetle?

How many Lambeosaurus have pink spots?

Find five
sandwiches hidden
on the page.

Which Minmi is
wearing glasses?

Look for the
dinosaur with an
unusual tail.

Who has a
beetle on their
back?

74

Spinosaurus has a large sail on its back like this one. Look for four.

Find ten fish to feed all these hungry dinosaurs.

How many swimming creatures like this one are there?

Can you see this striped Allosaurus inside the main shape?

Here are three types of creatures—Trilobites, Nautilus, and Ammonites.

Trilobites were beetle-like creatures. Make the ones with antennae brown.

Ammonites had spiral shells. Make them blue.

Find four black-eyed Nautilus. Make them pink and white.

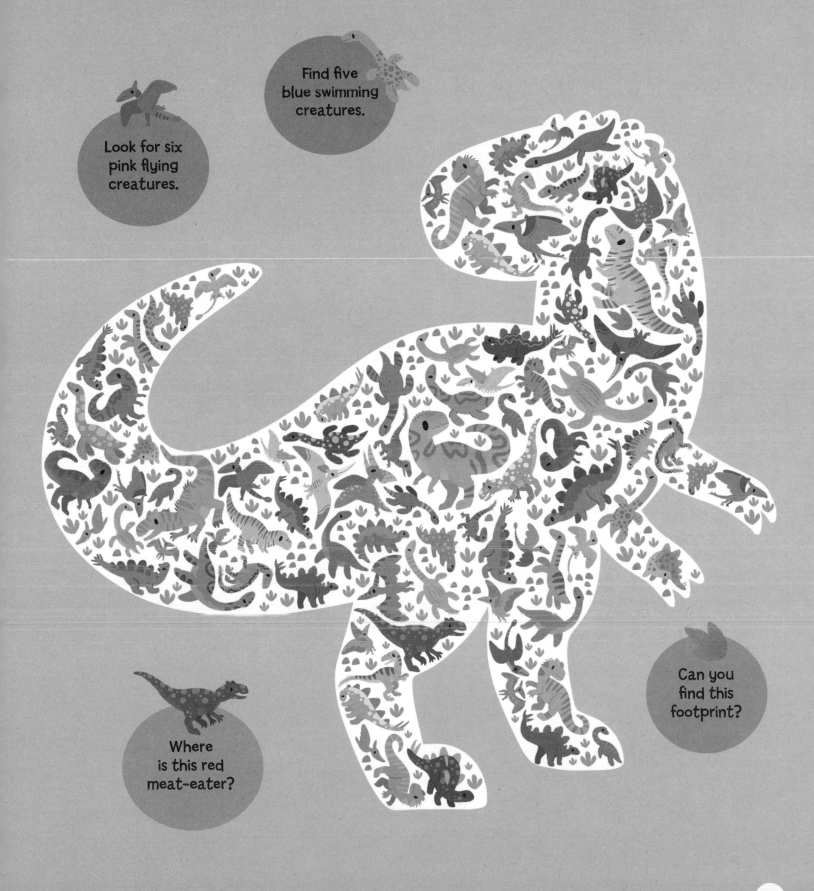

Look for six pink flying creatures.

Find five blue swimming creatures.

Where is this red meat-eater?

Can you find this footprint?

Where is the pesky mosquito?

Find eight apples.

How many hats are there?

How many striped tails are there?

78

Which of these
Muttaburrasaurus
has tiger stripes?

Which one looks
like a zebra?

Find the dinosaur
that has been
to a party.

How many have
green eyes?

79

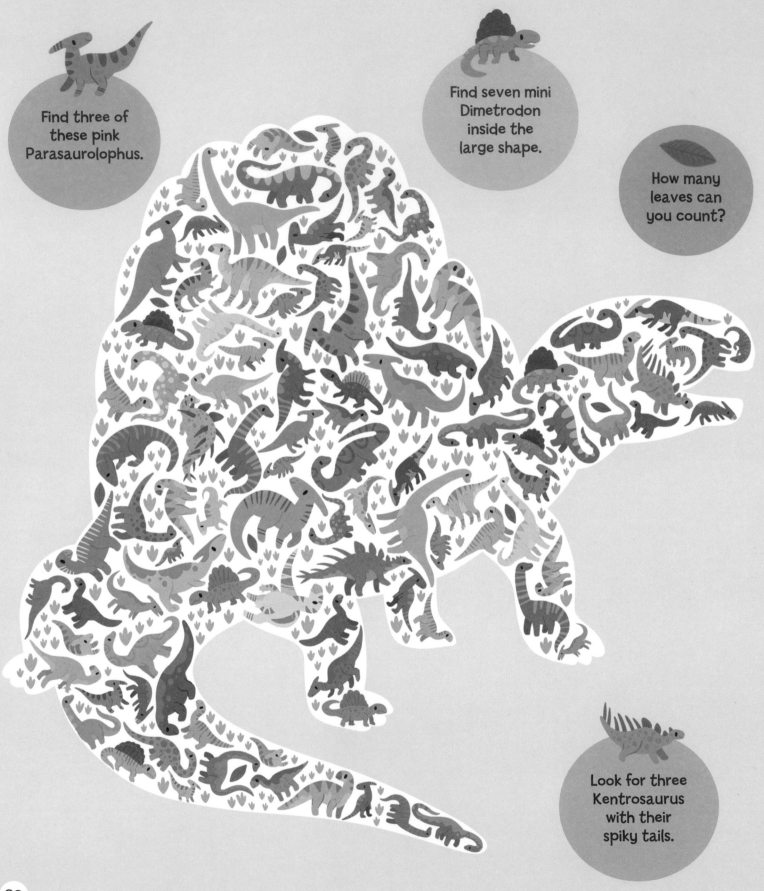

Find three of these pink Parasaurolophus.

Find seven mini Dimetrodon inside the large shape.

How many leaves can you count?

Look for three Kentrosaurus with their spiky tails.

80

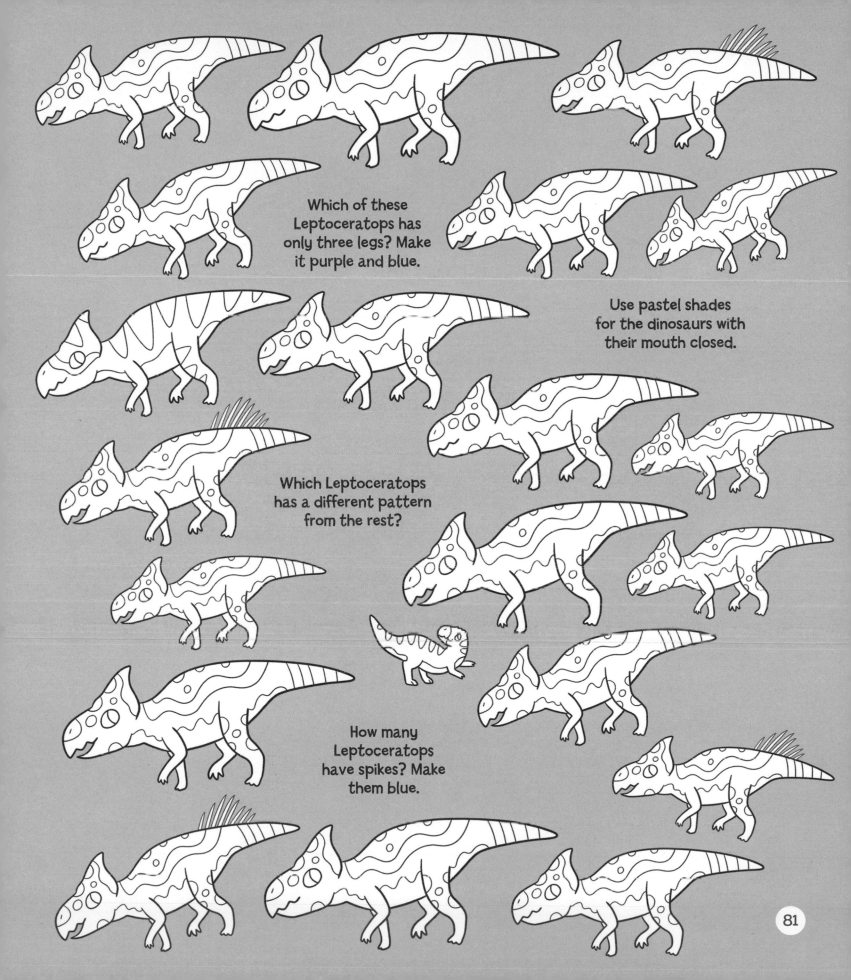

Which of these Leptoceratops has only three legs? Make it purple and blue.

Use pastel shades for the dinosaurs with their mouth closed.

Which Leptoceratops has a different pattern from the rest?

How many Leptoceratops have spikes? Make them blue.

Use blue and green on the bird-like Deinonychus.

How many dinosaurs have scarves?

Give red spots to three dinosaurs.

How many long-legged Gallimimus are running around?

82

83

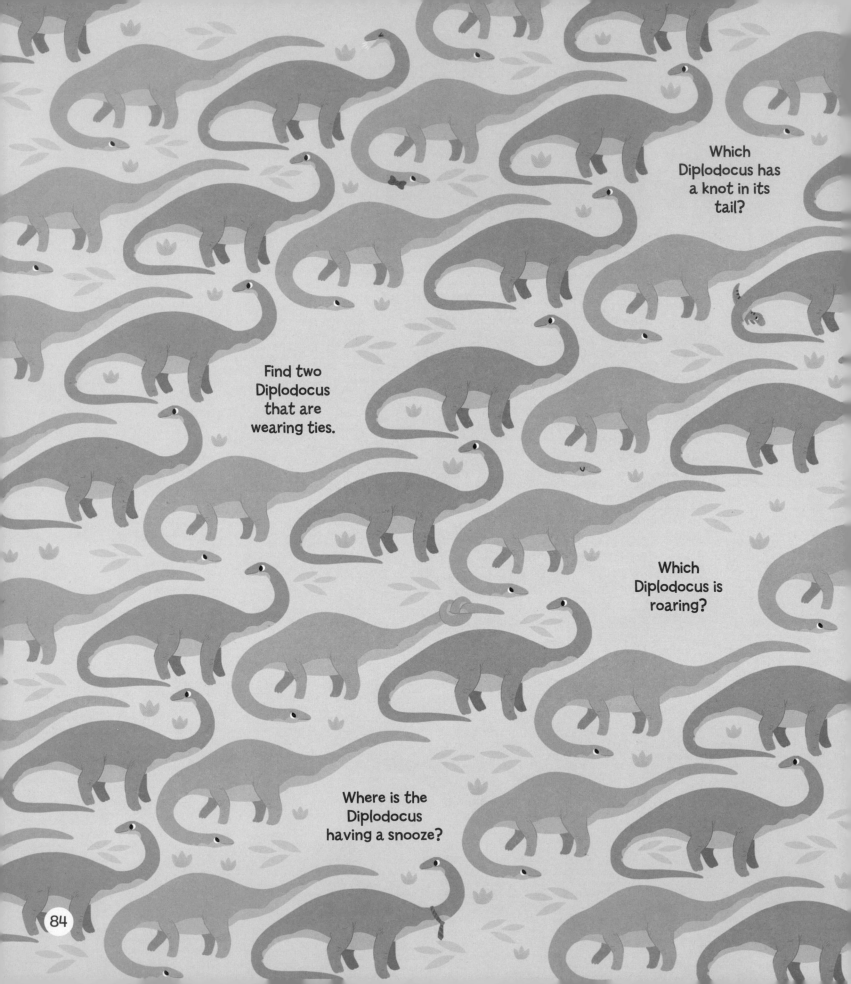

Which Diplodocus has a knot in its tail?

Find two Diplodocus that are wearing ties.

Which Diplodocus is roaring?

Where is the Diplodocus having a snooze?

84

How many purple creatures are there?

Find two orange club-tailed dinosaurs.

Where is this Diplodocus with the curly tail inside the big shape?

How many Triceratops are there?

PRONUNCIATION GUIDE

Allosaurus: AL-oh-SORE-us
Ammonite: AM-oh-nite
Ankylosaurus: an-KIH-loh-SORE-us
Apatosaurus: ah-PAT-oh-SORE-us
Archaeopteryx: ARK-ee-OPT-er-ix

Baryonyx: BAH-ree-ON-icks
Brachiosaurus: BRAH-kee-oh-SORE-us

Camarasaurus: KAM-uh-ruh-SORE-us
Centrosaurus: SEN-tro-SORE-us
Corythosaurus: KOH-rith-oh-SORE-us

Deinonychus: dy-NON-ik-us
Dimetrodon: dy-MET-roh-don
Dimorphodon: dy-MOR-foh-don
Diplodocus: dip-LOH-doh-kus

Elasmosaurus: el-LAZZ-moh-SORE-us
Eoraptor: EE-oh-RAP-tuhr
Euoplocephalus: you-OH-plo-KEF-ah-lus

Gallimimus: gal-uh-MY-mus

Hadrosaurus: HAD-ro-SORE-us

Ichthyosaurus: ICK-thee-oh-SORE-us
Iguanodon: ig-WAH-noh-don

Kentrosaurus: KEN-tro-SORE-us

Maiasaura: MY-ah-SORE-ah
Microraptor: MY-kroh-rap-tuhr
Minmi: MIN-mee

Nautilus: NAW-tih-lus

Oviraptor: OH-vee-RAP-tuhr

Pachycephalosaurus:
  pak-ee-SEF-ah-lo-SORE-us
Parasaurolophus: PA-ra-sore-OL-off-us
Protarchaeopteryx: PRO-tark-ee-OPT-er-ix
Protoceratops: PRO-toh-SEH-rah-tops
Pteranodon: teh-RAH-no-don
Pterosaur: TEH-roh-sore

Ramphorhynchus: RAM-foh-RINK-us

Spinosaurus: SPINE-oh-SORE-us
Stegosaurus: STEG-oh-SORE-us
Styracosaurus: sty-RACK-oh-SORE-us
Suchomimus: SOOK-oh-mim-us

Torosaurus: TOR-oh-SORE-us
Triceratops: try-SEH-ra-tops
Trilobite: TRY-lo-bite
Tyrannosaurus rex: ty-RAN-oh-SORE-us REX

Velociraptor: veh-LOSS-ee-rap-tuhr

Answers

The hidden T. rex on every page.

Page 3

- Mitten.
- Flower matching stripes.
- Twin.

Page 4

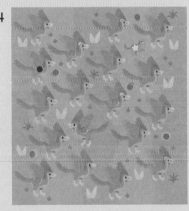

- Archaeopteryx with an orange head crest.
- Three dinosaurs with their tongues sticking out.
- Five fossils.
- Archaeopteryx facing the other way.

Page 5

- Three spiral ammonites.
- Three Parasaurolophus.
- Two blue and green Stegosaurus.
- Two purple and blue Triceratops.

Page 6

- Dinosaur with a saddle.
- Six matching dinosaurs.
- Dinos like me.

Page 7

- Green, flying friend.
- Sleepy dinosaur.
- Ten yellow flowers.
- Flying Pterosaur with the long tail.

Page 8

- Eight eggs.
- Six purple fish.
- Dinosaur with the fewest spots.
- Creature with a triangle shape on the tip of its tail.

Page 9

- T. rex covered in polka dots.
- Five T. rex wearing mittens.
- A mighty creature with blue eyes.
- A bone unlike any of the others.

Page 10

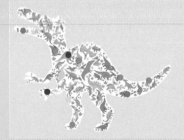

- Two purple Suchomimus.
- Two purple, flying Pteranodon.
- Two red matching dinosaurs.
- Three orange Ankylosaurus.

Page 11

- Wannanosaurus twin.
- Three spotted dinos.
- Four dinos with hats.

Page 12

- Allosaurus with blue eyes.
- Allosaurus with no teeth.
- Allosaurus carrying a potplant.
- Six Allosaurus with stripes.

Page 13

- A spiky tail.
- Seven have caught a fish.
- Pterosaur with a forked tail.
- Two with a red crest.

Page 14

- Yellow Pachycephalosaurus with blue stripes.
- Seven dinosaurs with green markings.
- Dinosaur with a crash helmet on.
- An animal with very large teeth.

Page 15

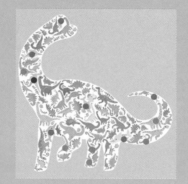

- One matching Gallimimus.
- Small pink Brachiosaurus.
- Six swimming Ichthyosaurus.
- Six Brachiosaurus with spots.

Page 16

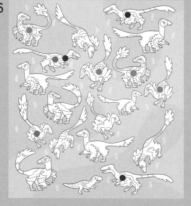

- Three Utahraptors showing their teeth.
- Spotted Utahraptors.
- The Utahraptor with its tongue out.

Page 17

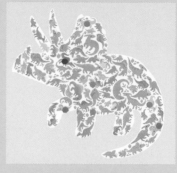

- The only red Spinosaurus in the crowd.
- Two matching Parasaurolophus.
- Two green spotted Triceratops.
- Two cycads.

Page 18

- A Stegosaurus in socks.
- A dinosaur in a bow-tie.
- The biggest dragonfly on the page.
- The horned rhinoceros beetle.

Page 19

- An Ankylosaurus with an unusual tail club.
- An Ankylosaurus wearing a watch.
- The Ankylosaurus with purple spikes.
- Seven Ankylosaurus with green legs.

Page 20

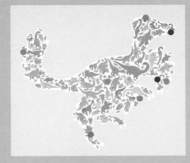

- Two of these green sauropods.
- Two dino heads.
- Spotted twin.
- Three blue Microraptors.

Page 21

- The smallest.
- One sail-backed Dimetrodon.
- The reptiles that look like me.
- Four large creatures with pointy teeth.

Page 22

- Spotted Triceratops.
- Stegosaurus wearing a hat.
- Dinosaur with a long, striped neck.
- Six dinosaurs with striped tails.

Page 23

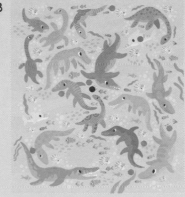

- One of us going the opposite way.
- Six green fish.
- My mother.
- Toy submarine.

Page 24

- Big Brachiosaurus with the shortest tail.
- Dinosaur wearing glasses.
- Little Dryosaurus with stripes on its back.
- A baby Brachiosaurus next to its mother.

Page 25

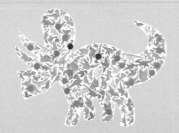

- Two matching blue Pachycephalosaurus.
- Three spotted Parasaurolophus.
- Six flying reptiles with their beaks open.
- Eight small Torosaurus.

Page 26

- Tails like mine.
- Four toothed creatures.
- Spotty flyers.

Page 27

- Ten tiny Eoraptors running around.
- The dinosaur with something in his mouth.
- Triceratops wearing a scarf.
- Buzzy bee.

Page 28

- Little lizard.
- Missing hat.
- Banana peel.
- Five other fish like me.

Page 29

- Spiky Centrosaurus.
- Torosaurus with a missing nose horn.
- Torosaurus wearing a party hat.
- Torosaurus with different markings from the rest.

Page 30

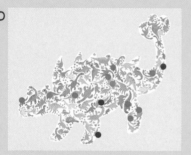

- Three blue dinosaurs just like this one.
- The green, spiky-tailed Kentrosaurus.
- Eight spotted creatures.
- Dinosaur wearing a coat.

Page 31

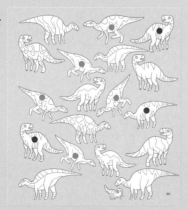

- Dinos with striped bellies.
- Five running dinosaurs.

Page 32

- Four green Acrocanthosaurus.
- Long-necked sauropods.
- Two other Carnotaurus with horns.
- Dinosaur with long, green spikes on its head.

Page 33

- Curliest tail.
- Yellow head crest.
- Two dinosaurs that are exactly the same.
- Someone with an orange eye.

Page 34

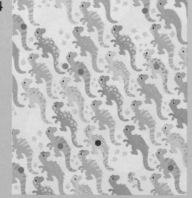

- Allosaurus with an eyeglass.
- Footprint different from the rest.
- Six Allosaurus have red stripes.
- Allosaurus with red spots.

Page 35

- The only purple flying creature.
- Suchomimus with a fish in its mouth.
- Corythosaurus with a striped tail.
- The yellow, swimming reptile with a long neck.

Page 36

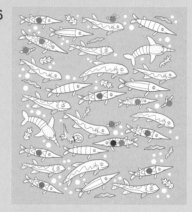

- Fish swimming the wrong way.
- Three spotted fish.
- Fish with triangular markings.
- Striped coral.

Page 37

- Two dinosaurs that look just like me.
- The blue, sleeping sauropod.
- Two matching pink sauropods.
- My twin.

Page 38

- My phone.
- The dino who has been hiding in the bushes.
- The dino that has been dancing.
- There are more dinosaurs with spikes.

Page 39

- Three dinosaurs with yellow beaks.
- Six Deinonychus have their mouths open.
- The Deinonychus with a crown on its head.
- Fallen feather.

Page 40

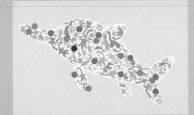

- The only flying creature in the main shape.
- Two Kronosaurus matching this one.
- Nine Ichthyosaurus.
- Six pink nautilus.

Page 41

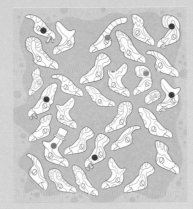

- Five dinosaurs are munching leaves.
- Dinosaur with a hidden heart pattern.
- Fanciest-hat wearer.
- The dinosaur with the longest head crest.

Page 42

- The spiky dinosaur with a heart-shaped club tail.
- The dinosaur with the biggest spikes.
- The flying dinosaur with the diamond tail.
- The dinosaurs with striped legs.

Page 43

- The dinosaur with a lizard lunch.
- The dinosaur waving a magic wand.
- The dinosaur with spots and no stripes.
- Two tiny lizards that look exactly the same.

Page 44

- The odd beak out.
- The Ornithocheirus wearing a hat.
- The Ornithocheirus that has caught a fish.
- The boot-wearer.

Page 45

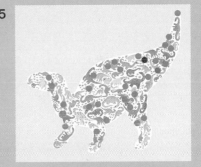

- The dinosaur that is munching on leaves.
- Eighteen fish.
- A dinosaur with its tail in a twist.
- Ten dinosaurs that have a neck frill.

Page 46

- The Velociraptor with unusual eyes.
- The Velociraptor with a feathered head crest.
- Four lizards have a curly tail.

Page 47

- Three Protoceratops have tail spikes.
- The sleeping Ankylosaurus who is missing its club.
- Nine flying Rhamphorynchus.
- The dinosaur that is clowning around.

Page 48

- The tiny flyer.
- A tail with a bow on it.
- The lost pencil.
- The running dinosaur.

Page 49

- Five eggs are pink.
- The Maiasaura with a bow on its tail.
- The baby heading in the wrong direction.
- The Maiasaura with a flower on its head.

Page 50

- Six Stegosaurus.
- Thirteen Elasmosaurus.
- The Elasmosaurus wearing shades.
- Two matching sauropods.

Page 51

- The joker wearing a disguise.
- The Apatosaurus with the curliest tail.

Page 52

- The Deinonychus who has no tail feathers.
- Five red Deinonychus.
- A small Deinonychus who has a purple beak.
- A dinosaur with a different-shaped head crest.

Page 53

- Iguanodon wearing gloves.
- A flying creature with a hat on.
- A small furry mammal.
- Seven flying creatures.

Page 54

- The Lambeosaurus with spots instead of stripes.
- Nine dinosaurs have a plain head crest.
- Dinosaur with a spotted head crest.
- A dropped watch.

Page 55

- Two Brachiosaurus with very long necks.
- Two matching Kentrosaurus.
- Pink Kentrosaurus with green spikes.
- Three Triceratops with pink stripes.

Page 56

- Four dinos wearing boots.
- A slightly different leaf.
- The dinosaur wearing shades.
- Feathers.

Page 57

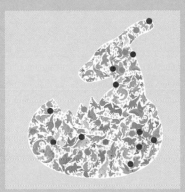

- Eleven eggs.
- Five blue Triceratops.
- The baby just hatched from its egg.
- Seven orange flyers.

Page 58

- A message in a bottle.
- A six-gilled shark.
- A fish that looks like me.
- Six fish that look like me.

Page 59

- The Euoplocephalus with missing shoulder spikes.
- Three Euoplocephalus have a green club.
- The stylish scarf wearer.
- Four dinosaurs with a spotted underside.

Page 60

- Four blue sail-backed Spinosaurus.
- Orange plant-eater.
- Four cycads.
- A tiny fish.

Page 61

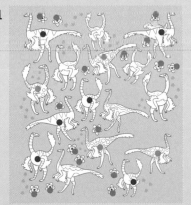

- Six Ornithomimus have striped legs.
- Four Ornithomimus have spots.
- Flowers.

Page 62

- The dinosaur with a party hat.
- The dinosaurs with two spikes on their tails.
- The babies.
- The Stegosaurus with plates down their backs.

Page 63

- Six snails.
- Skating dinosaur.
- The sign points to a volcano.
- A dinosaur carrying a parasol.

Page 64

- Three Rhamphorhynchus with yellow wings.
- Rhamphorhynchus with orange eyes.
- Rhamphorhynchus carrying a stick.
- The Rhamphorhynchus missing its sharp teeth.

Page 65

- Four Utahraptors with feathered arms.
- A hidden feather.
- Red Pteranodon.
- Four yellow Stegosaurus.

Page 66

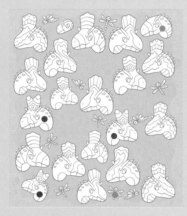

- Three pointed crests.
- The dragonfly with extra wings.
- The Cryolophosaurus without a crest.

Page 67

- The dragonfly.
- A dinosaur with a striped tail.
- The Pterosaur which has caught a fish.
- Five horned Styracosaurus.

Page 68

- Five little lizards.
- Dinosaur with a toy dino.
- Dino with a blue tail club.
- A nest with four eggs in it.

Page 69

- The Cryptoclidus with an S shape on its back.
- The hiding turtle.
- Four fish.
- Three Cryptoclidus have stripes.

Page 70

- Seven spiky Kentrosaurus.
- Three green Pachycephalosaurus.
- The dinosaur with no tail.
- A cycad.

Page 71

- Dinosaurs with striped legs.
- Skating dinosaur.
- Dinosaurs with two spikes on their tails.
- The dinosaur with something stuck on one of its spikes.

Page 72

- The Lambeosaurus with no head crest.
- Seven have leg stripes.
- The beetle.
- Six Lambeosaurus have pink spots.

Page 73

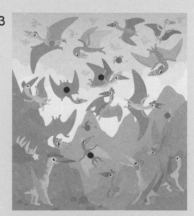

- Three yellow-crested flyers.
- My sister with a beak like mine.
- Three tiny long-tailed pterosaurs.
- The creature with fancy footwear.

Page 74

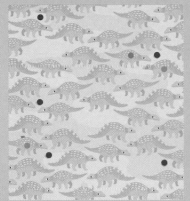

- Five hidden sandwiches.
- Minmi wearing glasses.
- The dinosaur with an unusual tail.
- The dinosaur with a beetle on its back.

Page 75

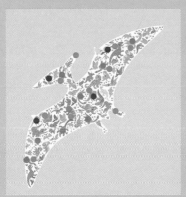

- Four Spinosaurus.
- Ten fish.
- Eight swimming creatures.
- Striped Allosaurus inside the main shape.

Page 76

- Trilobites with antennae.
- Ammonites.
- Four black-eyed Nautilus.

Page 77

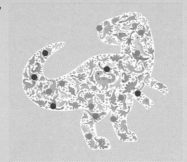

- Five blue swimming creatures.
- Six pink flying creatures.
- Red meat-eater.
- Footprint.

Page 78

- Pesky mosquito.
- Eight apples.
- Six hats.
- Six striped tails.

Page 79

- Muttaburrasaurus with tiger stripes.
- The one that looks like a zebra.
- The dinosaur that has been to a party.
- Six have green eyes.

Page 80

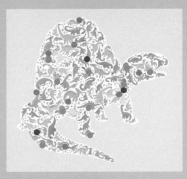

- Three pink Parasaurolophus.
- Seven mini Dimetrodon.
- Eight leaves.
- Three Kentrosaurus.

Page 81

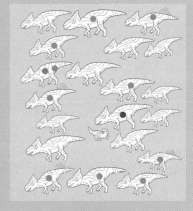

- Leptoceratops with only three legs.
- Dinosaurs with their mouth closed.
- The Leptoceratops with a different pattern.
- Four Leptoceratops have spikes.

Page 82

- The bird-like Deinonychus.
- Four dinosaurs have scarves.
- Six long-legged Gallimimus.

Page 83

- A pile of dino dung.
- The dino wearing a jacket and tie.
- Four furry caterpillars.
- An oviraptor with purple feet.

Page 84

- Diplodocus with a knot in its tail.
- Two Diplodocus wearing ties.
- Roaring Diplodocus.
- The Diplodocus having a snooze.

Page 85

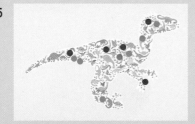

- There are five purple creatures.
- Two orange club-tailed dinosaurs.
- Diplodocus with the curly tail.
- There are four Triceratops.

Did you spot me on every page?